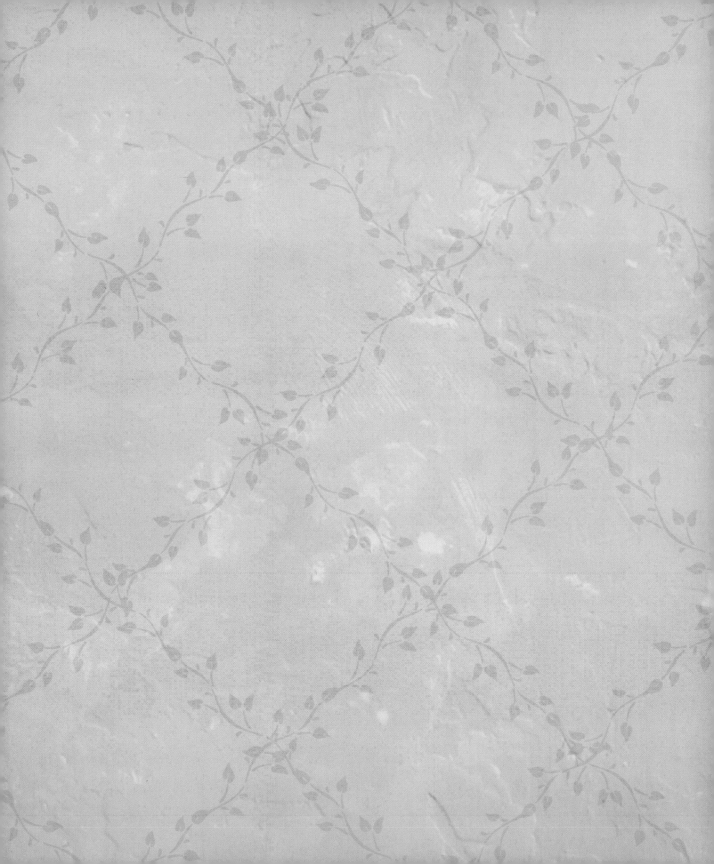

GARDEN MOMENT
Getaways

EMILIE BARNES
Paintings by SUSAN RIOS

HARVEST HOUSE PUBLISHERS
EUGENE, OREGON

GARDEN MOMENT
Getaways

Text Copyright © 2008 by Bob and Emilie Barnes
Artwork Copyright © 2008 by Susan Rios
Published by Harvest House Publishers
Eugene, Oregon 97402
www.harvesthousepublishers.com

ISBN-13: 978-0-7369-2018-6
ISBN-10: 0-7369-2018-8

Design and production by Garborg Design Works, Savage, Minnesota

Unless otherwise indicated, all Scripture quotations are taken from the New King James Version. Copyright ©1982 by Thomas Nelson, Inc. Used by permission. All rights reserved.

Verses marked NIV are taken from the HOLY BIBLE, NEW INTERNATIONAL VERSION®. NIV®. Copyright©1973, 1978, 1984 by the International Bible Society. Used by permission of Zondervan. All rights reserved.

Original artwork by Susan Rios. For more information regarding artwork featured in this book, please contact:

> Susan Rios, Incorporated
> 15335 Morrison Street, Suite 102
> Sherman Oaks, CA 91403
> (818) 995-7467 www.susanriosinc.com

Harvest House Publishers has made every effort to trace the ownership of all poems and quotes. In the event of a question arising from the use of a poem or quote, we regret any error made and will be pleased to make the necessary correction in future editions of this book.

Printed in Thailand

08 09 10 11 12 13 14 15 16 / IM / 10 9 8 7 6 5 4 3 2 1

I've learned to take a hurried part of my life, slow it down, plant the seeds, and watch with patient eyes to see the miracle of God's creation. I thank you who have helped me get here. And for all the readers who are ready for the getaway that only an afternoon in the garden can provide, I wish for you the blossoming of peace and great joy in all the seasons of your life.

—Emilie

A Getaway in
Every Garden

However big or small your garden is, if you allow nature to touch your spirit, gardening will bring returns of peace, satisfaction, and well-being for as long as you continue to wander the garden path.

—Norman H. Hansen

We enjoy the beauty of a garden when we look out the kitchen window or walk along a stone pathway. We enjoy it all the more when we allow the garden's beauty to infuse our lives.

In every season of the year, the garden pours forth gifts that feed us physically, spiritually, and emotionally. Every day the garden lavishes the gifts of serenity, fragrance, and flavor. My response is to say thank-you every time I am blessed with a garden moment or the bounty of a garden's offering. This gratitude reminds me that all this is a gift from above.

I invite you to enjoy the treasures of your own garden—spend your days and hours surrounded by the abundant and giving hand of nature. Share the joy, share the healing, share the offerings of your garden, and you will discover new ways to celebrate all that is around you in life.

Let's get away to some special garden moments as we journey through seasons of life together. May each moment transport you, transform you, and provide you with the gifts of that very first garden—peace and beauty.

Emilie

GARDEN OF
Healing

*And they heard the sound of the LORD God
walking in the garden in the cool of the day.*

THE BOOK OF GENESIS

Just as our gardens face the downtime of winter's slumber, we too experience times when we must wait, heal, and hope. It's good to take our cues from the cycle of nature. Let your body and soul heal from a busy year of errands, responsibilities, goals, dreams, and, yes—gardening!

My husband, Bob, tells me about visiting his beloved grandpa, PaPa, in Texas. The whole family would attend his PaPa's favorite country church. When the congregation started to sing "In the Garden," written by C. Austin Miles, PaPa's strong voice would join in boldly, with surprising strength: "I come to the garden alone, while the dew is still on the roses; and the voice I hear, falling on my ear, the Son of God discloses. And He walks with me, and He talks with me, and He tells me I am His own, and the joy we share as we tarry there, none other has ever known."

C. Austin Miles knew that the art of meditating on Scripture involves one's imagination. Instead of simply reading a passage, we must read it, close our eyes, and visualize the scene, perhaps even putting ourselves in the picture. He understood that there are times we all need comfort and healing; there are times we all need to meet with God in the garden for solace and strength.

That's what you can do as you approach your healing garden. You can bring all of your hurts and cares to God even when you don't know what to hope for anymore. You don't have to have the answers when you come to this garden. Take a quiet stroll through the walkways; stop for a moment of prayer on a bench. Pause and take in a view that in other seasons you might walk right by. Allow beauty to be a part of your healing journey. Don't be in a hurry because healing takes time.

Listen to the sounds of the garden, ones that you may have never heard before. It's amazing what you hear when you are quiet and still. When the sounds of hope and peace cover you, your own voice can join in boldly.

Your hurts and your wounds may be old or they may still be fresh. Use your garden or a community garden as a refuge where the healing process can begin.

To have complete satisfaction from flowers you must have time to spend with them. There must be rapport. I talk to them and they talk to me.

—Princess Grace of Monaco

Creating a Beautiful Outdoor Space

There is something very satisfying about having your own outdoor space, however small it may be (some of the most beautiful gardens occur in small spaces). There is no reason why you shouldn't plan and decorate your outdoor garden with as much care and thought as you would give the rooms inside your home.

Think about how you want to use your garden and what you want to include in it: seating areas, play areas, beds and borders, shrubs, vegetable plots, and storage. Decide on a style so the garden has an identity. You can also create impact using paint and stain on surfaces such as fences, walks, furniture, or pots to complement the planting. Stay flexible with your plan. Adjustments usually need to be made. Don't forget to include space devoted to flat surfaces such as lawns, walkways, and patios. Throughout your planning, keep in mind how much time you want to spend maintaining your garden.

Once a garden is in place, add finishing touches. Ornaments, arches, and pergolas can all be used to maximize the views, creating places of shade and sunshine and enhancing the overall layout of your garden. Adding lighting, sprinklers, and seating will extend your use of the outdoor space.

MY GARDEN IS MY HEALING PLACE,
A HOSPITAL WARD FOR NURSING MY WOUNDED SPIRIT.
WHENEVER WE MOVE AND LAND IN UNFAMILIAR
TERRITORY, THE FIRST THING I DO IS PUT GROWING
THINGS IN THE EARTH OF MY NEW YARD.

—CINDY CROSBY

Dream Pillows

*Encourage sweet sleep and sweet dreams for yourself and friends
with a homemade dream pillow. The ingredients can vary; each herb
is purported to have a particular effect. Whether or not this is true,
the aroma is certainly dreamy.*

½ cup hops (to encourage sleep)
⅛ cup lavender flowers (to make dreams pleasant)
2 tablespoons mugwort leaves (to instill dreams)
⅛ cup rosemary leaves (to help sleeper recall dreams)
⅛ cup thyme (to prevent nightmares)
⅛ cup rose petals (for dreams of love)

Blend ingredients and sew into small muslin pillows. Tuck
inside pillowcase at night. Or sew a pretty pillow with a little
pocket on the outside to hold the dream pillow. Give as a gift
with a card to explain.

Tips for the Gardener

One of the garden's many lessons relates to how creation is designed to heal itself.
The earth becomes richer and more fruitful if we fuel it with nutrients that *it* provides.
Simply amazing! Here are instructions for quick composting:

- To produce coarse compost in 1 to 2 months, use a 50-50 mixture of green and
  brown materials. Green materials include grass clippings and vegetable scraps.
  Brown materials include dead leaves, wood chips, or straw (not hay).
  For finer-textured compost, let the pile work for several more weeks.
- On open ground, build a pile roughly 3 feet in diameter with alternating 6-inch
  layers of green matter and brown matter.
- Once a week, mix and aerate the materials by moving the pile a few feet with a
  pitch fork. In dry weather hose the pile down to keep the pile as moist as a
  wrung-out sponge.
- Dig compost into beds or use it as a mulch.

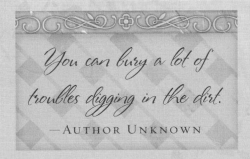

*You can bury a lot of
troubles digging in the dirt.*
—Author Unknown

GARDEN OF *Joy*

How good is man's life, the mere living!
How fit to employ all the heart and the soul
and the senses, forever in joy!

—ROBERT BROWNING

We expect joy to be about unlimited happiness and never-ending. Truly happiness and fun are a part of our lives, but they come and go with circumstances. Joy, on the other hand, is felt beyond our circumstances. It is an attitude that fills us and covers us when we face difficulties and when we encounter special moments. Joy grows from the heart, and it blossoms with the radiant colors of gratitude.

Let's follow the path of simplicity to the garden where our surroundings are lovely, inspiring, and filled with sounds and images that nurture joy. Place chimes throughout the yard and listen to the wind greet you as it rushes through the trees. Display a collection of antique birdhouses—not only will you enjoy the art of such designs but you will be blessed with the sounds of the birds who gather to feast and say thank you in song. One of my

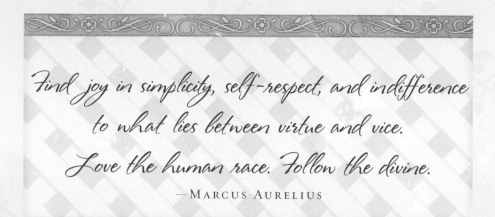

Find joy in simplicity, self-respect, and indifference to what lies between virtue and vice. Love the human race. Follow the divine.

—MARCUS AURELIUS

favorite garden inspirations is the sound of rushing water. Whether it is a nearby natural brook or a man-made fountain, water adds a lovely soundtrack of joy.

Interestingly, my sense of humor improves in the garden. My husband will attest to that. We laugh more easily when we're working together outdoors. Why not? I'm at peace. I use this time of hope to nurture my spiritual life in prayer. It's in the garden that God speaks to me. A thought, an idea, a dream—all are formed more readily when my mind is relaxed and I can plan for the future. Because of my faith in God, I have optimism for tomorrow.

Moments of contentment and times of pure delight are savored not only by the gardener but also by others who are welcomed to these cherished spaces. When we share our love and our sanctuaries with friends we know (and even those we just met), we are sharing moments of joy in the present and joyful memories in the years to come.

THE LESSON I HAVE THOROUGHLY LEARNT, AND WISH TO PASS ON TO OTHERS, IS TO KNOW THE ENDURING HAPPINESS THAT THE LOVE OF A GARDEN GIVES.

—GERTRUDE JEKYLL

Fountain of Joy

"Hope springs eternal," so why not bring a water feature into your garden? Whether it's the sound of a small trickling wall fountain or the bubbling of a large standing one, there's nothing like the sound of water to refresh the soul and fill your heart with hope.

Minimizing evaporation is the key to creating an effective water feature. It's easier in some states than others. The drier the air and the more vigorous the water's motion, the faster water evaporates. Yet even modest spill fountains can be as cooling as powerful sprays and thundering cascades, and their softer music can be more pleasing to the ear.

There are so many ways to add water to your garden. Go online, search out your home improvement store, look in your yellow pages—spend some time figuring out exactly what meets your needs because once you decide, a water feature will be with you for a long time.

Tips for the Gardener

Keep those outdoor gardening tools looking like new—no more rust or clinging dirt the next time you pull them out of the shed. Make yourself a garden tool container. Fill a large galvanized trough or other container with sand to 1 inch from top. Pour in about ¼ cup of motor oil and stir (sand should have a slightly moist texture). When returning tools to trough, wipe them with a rag. The sand will keep tools clean and sharp, and the oil will keep them rust free.

Such a commotion under the ground,
When March called, "Ho, there! ho!"
Such spreading of rootlets far and wide,
Such whisperings to and fro!

"Are you ready?" the Snowdrop asked,
"'Tis time to start, you know."
"Almost, my dear!" the Scilla replied,
"I'll follow as soon as you go."

Then "Ha! ha! ha!" a chorus came
Of laughter sweet and low,
From millions of flowers under the ground,
Yes, millions beginning to grow.

—RALPH WALDO EMERSON
From Flower Chorus

GARDEN OF
Hope

Go not abroad for happiness.
For see it is a flower that blooms at thy door.

—MINOT J. SAVAGE

I love a garden. What a relief to have a place where the trees and plants cleanse the air. A garden is a place where I can "feel." It's a wonderful relief from all the bad news, the noisy traffic, the hurry and anxiety of life. No wonder our spirits are lifted the moment we wander a garden path. Oh, I know I can't stay here all day; there's work to be done. And I'll get it done one way or another. But it's here that God speaks to me. It's here that I can build up my hope to live another day, a month, a year. It's here that my senses rejoice and my sense of wonder is awakened.

The garden is where my senses come alive and I can rejoice more freely. I am able to notice little things I normally never see. I hear sounds that are not in my usual experience. There's something about being in the midst of God's creation that elicits hope. And why not? It's the simple things that give life to our living.

Most garden dreams thrive on hope. And gardeners, as a group, are the most hopeful people I know. It takes a measure of hope to make even the simplest beginning—to buy a pot, a bag of soil, a few shrubs, and a packet of seeds. It takes a hopeful spirit to see anemones and chrysanthemums in a strip of undecorated sod or bare dirt, to envision daffodils when the eye sees only snow—even to expect that a scrawny little bunch of leaves in a new pot will choose to grow and flower.

It takes hope to start a garden. But the garden itself is what really teaches you how to hope. A sense of faith and possibility grows in a gardener's heart every year as she watches the green veil grace once-bare branches or he sees a raked plot of plain ground suddenly explode with busy, purposeful growth.

Even when disappointments appear or this year's growth isn't as good as we would have wished, there's always next year. This is the gift of hope.

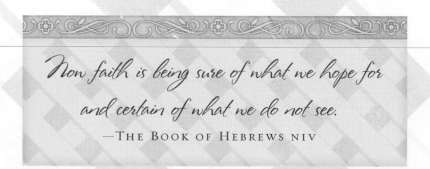

Now faith is being sure of what we hope for and certain of what we do not see.
—THE BOOK OF HEBREWS NIV

Flower Bed-Making Essentials

To add interest to garden beds, consider these ideas:

Angle.

How does the bed look from different areas of the garden—from paths, patios, or other gathering places? Angle the bed to get a good view from priority locations.

Shape.

A bed in the shape of a circle, a square, or an octagon looks formal, while one with a freeform shape has a casual look. Experiment by laying a hose on the ground and adjusting the curves.

Height.

To add visual interest to a level bed, mound soil in the center or at one end to create a gentle slope. Consider creating an elevated stage for an art object or accent plant.

Edging.

If you want your edging to look crisp, use brick or other pavers. If you want it soft and informal, you can plant billowing perennials to accent the edges of the bed.

Accents.

A shapely border, a single well-placed piece of garden art, or a good accent plant makes the perfect finishing touch when it rises above lower plantings.

Color and texture.

For the heart of your beds, choose some permanent year-round plants. Consult your local nursery to select those that will do well in your particular climate zone.

O Spring-time sweet!
The whole Earth smiles,
thy coming to greet.
—Author Unknown

A Handy Hint

The same basic ingredients you use for potpourri can become the base for fragranced items throughout your home. Your potpourri mixture, crushed and stuffed into little muslin or calico bags, can serve as sachets in drawers and closets. For an extra-pretty sachet, make little lace hearts lined with tulle or netting and fill with potpourri, or wrap a little potpourri in a lace handkerchief and tie with a narrow ribbon.

TIPS FOR THE GARDENER

How to Water Trees

- Build watering basins. Mound soil berms around young trees to concentrate water on the root zone. Form the main berm just outside the tree's dripline; make a second berm 4 to 6 inches from the trunk to keep water off it.
- Use soaker hoses. These porous hoses ooze water along their length. For a large tree, coil a 50- to 75-foot hose out to the dripline.
- Irrigate the roots. Deep-root irrigators are hose-end devices with forked or needlelike shafts that inject water into the root zone of a mature tree, 12 to 24 inches below the surface. Insert the shaft into the soil along the drip line. After giving that spot a good soaking, move the irrigator to another spot along the drip line.

GARDENING IS THE ART THAT USES
FLOWERS AND PLANTS AS PAINT,
AND THE SOIL AND SKY AS CANVAS.

— ELIZABETH MURRAY

GARDEN OF *Meditation*

More things are wrought by prayer
than this world dreams of.

—ALFRED LORD TENNYSON

*T*he garden is a wonderful location to be still and think about the big issues in life. It is the best place for peaceful moments of contemplation. When spring arrives, new growth is taking place, the days are longer, and the sun is warmer—the flowers, bees, and birds seem to beckon us to take a moment to appreciate, to savor, to pray, to ponder.

What a powerful force in life is our daily prayer. There's something about the small plot of ground called a garden that releases our creativity while we communicate with the Creator of all gardens—God.

The garden has a soothing effect on my whole body. When I meditate in the garden, it seems as though time stands still. It makes me feel young again; the child in me becomes aglow—I feel cleansed and refreshed. I find if I have some plaques or statues along my paths to remind me of a higher purpose, the experience is even richer.

During this time don't plan to go out and work (no planting, no weeding). Allow the experience to be only about your thoughts, praise, prayers, dreams… and the stillness of the yard. It is tempting to prune a rose bush or pull a weed, but give your purpose of meditation equal time and effort. The garden is more than happy to be a place of pure rest for you. Savor it.

> See! The winter is past; the rains are over and gone. Flowers appear on the earth; the season of singing has come, the cooing of doves is heard in our land.
> —The Song of Solomon NIV

Room with a View—Your Porch

Hanging baskets are a wonderful way to expand your garden to the porch and porticos. Fabulous ferns and masses of brilliant impatiens have long been favorites to add color to difficult spaces. Look at hanging containers as a potential garden, just as you would a flower bed. They can provide a variety of colors, textures, and shapes and become a focal point to enrich your home.

When choosing a container, choose one that can be suspended easily and is strong enough to hold the weight of soil, water, and plants. When deciding on the basket, think about plants to go into it. If it does not hold much soil, the plants need to be shallow-rooted to grow properly. Purchase the appropriate basket for the plant requirements or the appropriate plants for the container.

Place your hanging basket where you would love to have color but can't find a way to get it there. Turn your hanging baskets into something special with a creative container and enjoy hanging them around.

> The greatest gift of the garden is the restoration of the five senses.
> —Hanna Rion

Breathe In and Relax

As prayers and meditations are lifted up, so are the inspiring scents of a garden. Here are two great ways to bring the aromatic wonder of your garden into your home.

Roses upon Roses Bath Sachet

½ cup quick oats
½ cup dried rose petals
¼ cup dried rose geranium leaves
½ cup table salt
2 teaspoons rose oil
5 small muslin bags in shades of pink
   and rose

Mix ingredients in a bowl. Put mixture into bags and tie with twine or waterproof ribbon, making a bow or loop. After you have filled the tub, swish the sachet through hot water a few times or hang it under the running water as the tub fills. Hang the sachet on the faucet to dry. It can be used several times. For guests, place bags in a basket in your bathroom with a little note about how to use them. Try different combinations of herbs and oils such as rosemary with lavender oil or pine oil.

Peppermint Foot Bath

8 cups water
1 tablespoon table salt
5 sprigs dried peppermint (or another kind
   of mint, rosemary, or lemon verbena)

Boil water. Add table salt and peppermint. Let stand until water is warm and comfortable. Pour into a bowl and soak your feet 10 to 20 minutes. Rinse with cold water and apply lotion.

TIPS FOR THE GARDENER

Walls and gates are fantastic elements that help create an eye-popping outdoor landscape. An old-type gate welcomes visitors to the patio, while warm stone and stucco walls and a flagstone pathway emphasize the feel you would like to reflect in your yard.

Don't let limited space hinder your design of your garden. Small spaces often are the most rewarding. They require little maintenance, and the upkeep of plants, shrubs, and flowers is limited.

GARDEN OF
Hospitality

Let us be grateful to people who make us happy;
they are the charming gardeners who make our souls blossom.

—MARCEL PROUST

*I*f I ever wanted my granddaughter Christine's attention, all I had to do was to invite her over to share tea with me in our garden. Often she brought one of her girlfriends to share in the joy of our special ritual of teatime. I can think of no joy greater than extending the hospitality of my garden and my love for tea with my granddaughter.

There's something about the ceremony of brewing and sipping tea that soothes and settles everyone. Set aside a special place in the garden just for such an activity. I had two favorite places: one on the deck around the pond and waterfall and the other on the top deck of our tree house. Each was such a perfect setting.

I would have Christine help me with all the tea props: a card table, a lacy tablecloth, a few napkins, some plates, cups and saucers, and, of course, some recently made scones, cookies, or sweet breads. When your guests help set the table, they feel it really is their tea party.

There is no greater joy than to express hospitality in your own backyard sanctuary.

The sharing garden lets you have time—just you and your children or grandchildren—to hear what is important to them. Some of our fondest memories have come from these precious times together. These moments have been fabulous for bonding our separate generations. When we are together, we always think back to those minutes or hours we spent in the garden. "Remember when the squash were so big or the roses seemed to bloom forever? I just loved picking a basketful of navel oranges." These are fond memories that would not have occurred without the benefits of a garden.

Many of you live in the city and don't have the benefit of strolling together in your garden. However, you can take a few minutes' drive to get out of town to where there are farms that invite you in to pick corn, strawberries, watermelons, or pumpkins, and even choose and cut down your Christmas tree. Or how about volunteering together in a larger city garden? Be creative and think outside of the box.

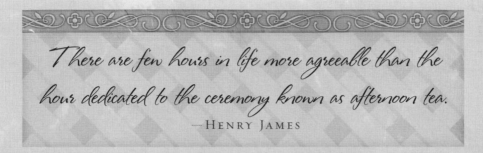

There are few hours in life more agreeable than the hour dedicated to the ceremony known as afternoon tea.

—HENRY JAMES

Brewing a Cup of Tea to Share

Empty the teakettle and refill it with freshly drawn cold water. Put the kettle on to boil. While the kettle is heating, pour hot water into the teapot to warm it. Ceramic (china, porcelain, stoneware) or glass teapots work best. Tea brewed in a metal teapot may have a metallic taste.

Pour the hot water out of the teapot. Measure a spoonful of loose tea for each cup desired into the warmed (but empty) teapot, plus one extra spoonful for the pot. (Most teapots hold 5 to 6 cups.) If you are using tea bags, use a bag less than the desired number of cups. Put the lid back on the pot.

As soon as the kettle comes to a rolling boil, remove it from the heat. Overboiling causes the water to lose oxygen, and the resulting brew will taste flat.

Pour boiling water into the teapot, cover, and let the tea brew from 3 to 6 minutes. Small tea leaves will take less time to brew than large ones.

Gently stir the tea before pouring it through a tea strainer into the teacups. If you used tea bags, remove them.

IF MAN HAS NO TEA IN HIM, HE IS INCAPABLE
OF UNDERSTANDING TRUTH AND BEAUTY.

—JAPANESE PROVERB

Basic Scones

Scones are quite simple to make, so I usually make my own. However, a packaged scone mix can also give you very good results. You can add all kinds of extras to scones, depending on your taste. Try cut-up apples, currants, ginger, oranges, almond flavoring, cinnamon, apricots, fresh blueberries, cranberries, or even chocolate chips.

> 2 cups flour
> 1 tablespoon baking powder
> 2 tablespoons sugar
> ½ teaspoon salt
> 6 tablespoons butter
> ½ cup buttermilk
> 1 lightly beaten egg

Mix dry ingredients. Cut in butter until mixture resembles coarse cornmeal. Make a well in the center and pour in buttermilk. If you don't have buttermilk, use regular milk. Mix until dough clings together and is a bit sticky—do not overmix. Turn out dough onto a floured surface and shape into a 6- to 8-inch round about 1½ inches thick. Quickly cut into pie wedges or use a large round biscuit cutter to cut circles. The secret of tender scones is a minimum of handling. Place on ungreased cookie sheet, making sure the sides of the scones don't touch each other. Brush with egg for a shiny, beautiful brown scone. Bake at 425° for 10 to 20 minutes or until light brown.

To transform this basic scone recipe into one for herb scones, add about 3 tablespoons fresh or 1 tablespoon dried herbs such as basil, thyme, or oregano. Serve with softened butter mixed with chopped herbs and a dash of lemon juice.

To pick a flower is so much more satisfying than just observing it, or photographing it...so in later years, I have grown in my garden as many flowers as possible for children to pick.

—Anne Scott James

Tips for the Gardener

Used tea leaves thrown into your rose garden can enrich the soil and act like peat moss, keeping plant roots moist. They also make a good mulch for garden plants, particularly for those that prefer an acid soil.

Garden of
Transformation

*Whatever good or bad fortune may come our way we can always
give it meaning and transform it into something of value.*

—Hermann Hesse

Gardens are continually changing. Somehow the plants we put in two years ago haven't done so well because the soil isn't right or the amount of sunshine is too great or too little. Or maybe plants that are growing well have taken over a corner that needs some variety. Not only is change required, but it is good and healthy. Transformation is all around us—in nature, in ourselves, in the life that is growing and blooming everywhere we look.

A good garden should evolve and change along with you and the needs and desires of your family. So don't feel bad if you decide to rip out the roses because you found a new love for grapes.

It doesn't mean that you throw away what you are removing, for you can move plants to a new location in the garden or you can share them with neighbors or friends. Anticipate this change early enough in the year that you can dig up the old plants while still dormant and not put them into shock because you waited too long into the spring.

One day, the gardener realizes that what she is doing out there is actually teaching herself to garden by performing a series of experiments. This is a pivotal moment in one's life.

—MARGARET ROACH

We should always be in the growing mode. Our lives are not planted in concrete. As we mature, we should become wiser and more open to change and growth and the wonders of new beginnings.

Be on the lookout to see what needs to be changed in your garden. Also, pay attention to the weeds that initially look innocent but can soon take over your favorite garden elements.

I have to do that with the issues of my life as well. When I try to break a bad habit or acquire a new good one, or I try to mend a broken relationship or build a new friendship, I must simply do what I know to do and then patiently wait for the results. I can't expect instant success, yet my experience in the garden tells me that the results will probably be worthwhile—I'll either achieve my objective, or I'll learn something I needed to learn about life.

Watch Them Grow

There is such joy in watching children and grandchildren grow. And they also find great happiness when they have a chance to watch a garden grow from mere seeds. Planting tomato seeds will not only be a fun science experiment but also a chance for those young and old to savor the process of transformation.

- Gardeners often start with tomato plants from the nursery. But a quick online search will produce a variety of seeds that are also available. And with seeds you get the added satisfaction of showing your children how a tiny seed turns into a juicy tomato.
- Tomato plants grown from seeds will require 6 to 8 weeks of care and nurturing before they can be planted outdoors. To begin, count backward from the final frost date in your area. After you transplant the seedlings to the garden, it takes about 100 days of water, sunshine, and TLC before you and your family can reap the ripe rewards. So mark your calendars, order your seeds, and away you go.

Emilie's Fresh Tomato Pasta Sauce with Basil

1 tablespoon olive oil

12 fresh tomatoes, cut up (leave the skin and seeds)

2 tablespoons fresh basil leaves, minced (or to taste)

4 or 5 garlic cloves, minced

½ teaspoon salt

2 tablespoons capers

Heat oil in deep frying pan, add all ingredients at once, and let simmer 10 to 15 minutes. Pour over hot angel hair pasta.

TIPS FOR THE GARDENER

Keep a file on hand for sharpening your tools. Buy a large one for shovels, hoes, and edgers and a smaller one for pruners and clippers. Hang on a nail near your tools and sharpen regularly. Nothing transforms hard labor into pure pleasure like a sharp tool.

Let us not become weary in doing good, for at the proper time we will reap a harvest if we do not give up.

—THE BOOK OF GALATIANS NIV

GARDEN OF
Remembrance

*Garden lessons are one of gardening's great joys—
equal almost to the joy of seeing one's dreams
gradually unfurl into green reality. I hope you will
make the time to be in the garden. I hope you will take
the time to be still and experience the paradise.*

—EMILIE BARNES

Gardens are a wonderful place in which to build or plant a tree to honor someone who has meant a lot to your family.

My husband's brother planted beautiful Eden climbing roses in honor of his mother on both sides of the white Cape Cod-style arbor he built. Each summer he sends us pictures showing how well "Mom's" roses are doing. It causes us to reflect back to the wonderful time we had with her, and it gives us a reason to pause and honor her with sweet memories.

Building a legacy and family traditions are what hold families together. Spending time remembering and reminiscing adds depth and meaning to our lives. When we share with our children and grandchildren about those who came before us, we are giving them stories to share when we are no longer on earth.

Everyone has a story. Don't forget to tell yours. In our younger days when we moved into a new home, we would plant a California sycamore tree to eventually provide shade for the front of our house. We flash back to those early days when the whole family gathered with Dad—shovel and mulch in hand—to dig the hole that would house our sycamore tree. Dad always dug the hole plenty deep, mixed the mulch with the soil, placed the tree in the hole, and filled in the dirt around the tree.

Our ceremony would include explaining the occasion the tree marked, making sure the whole family knew why that tree was so special. It was a remembering tree for our garden. As we drive by our old homes, we look out the windows at those trees and think back to when we had occasion to plant them. Some of them are now 40 to 50 years old. It is a nice feeling to see them standing strong and tall, gracing the current home's owner with shade and beauty.

JOY FOR THE
STURDY TREES;
FANNED BY EACH
FRAGRANT BREEZE.
—SAMUEL FRANCIS SMITH

The Value of Trees

Trees do much for the landscape of our homes and surroundings. It's hard to put a price on beauty, but property values of homes whose landscapes include mature trees are 5 to 20 percent higher than those without them.

Located where they'll shade windows from hot afternoon sun, mature trees can lower cooling costs by 10 to 40 percent. One such tree can cool a house as well as five average room air conditioners running 12 hours a day. Trees planted to block winter wind can reduce heating bills by 10 to 15 percent.

Check with your local nursery to see what they would recommend for your climate zone. Consider planting a tree to mark the birth or death of a special person or even to honor a significant life milestone. That tree will provide shelter, comfort, and beauty for years and will be a magnificent bit of creation to remind you of a loved one or an event.

Herb and Flower Salad

> 6 cups mixed baby greens
> 1 cup green leaf herbs (basil,
>   tarragon, Italian parsley,
>   chervil)
> ½ cup edible petals (nastur-
>   tium, daylily, calendula,
>   mint, pansy, sage, marigold,
>   rose, violet)

Toss greens and herbs together at the dinner table and arrange the edible petals on top for a decorative look. (Be sure to show your guest how colorful the salad looks.) Serve with Emilie's Olive Oil Dressing.

Emilie's Olive Oil Dressing
Makes 1½ cups

Mash together and put into a jar:
- 3 cloves pressed garlic
- 1 teaspoon salt
- ½ scant teaspoon pepper

Add and shake well:
- 1 cup olive oil
- ½ cup white vinegar
- ¼ cup lemon juice

Chill before spooning over salad greens.

Tips for the Gardener

Don't forget that many of your ornamentals in the garden are also edible.
A few are:

- *artichoke*—Violetto
- *basil*—Purple Ruffles and Green Ruffles
- *chives*—they look great in or out of bloom
- *Japanese red mustard*—leaves are very dramatic
- *lettuce*—Black-Seeded Simpson, Red Oak Leaf, Royal Oak Leaf
- *peas*—Dwarf Gray Sugar
- *peppers*—Super Chili, Golden Bell
- *Swiss chard*—Bright Lights has many colors

Guided by my heritage of a love of beauty and respect for strength—in search of my Mother's garden, I found my own.
—Alice Walker

Garden of
Sanctuary

Our life is like a garden,
And with God's loving care
It blossoms with the flowers
Of His blessings everywhere.

—Author Unknown

There are times when we just need to be by ourselves in a place where we can let down, think through important issues of life, talk to God in prayer, laugh out loud, and cry with bitter tears.

Create a sanctuary, a sacred place where you can retreat and be alone with God; a place that helps you hear His still small voice; a place that nurtures your soul and reminds you of the refuge of the Creator's love. Place a bench and table so you can take a cup of tea, a journal, and some note cards (write a note to a friend telling them that you prayed for them today) to your garden.

45

Several churches in our area have designed prayer gardens on their campuses so that the church members as well as community people can come and spend a delightful block of time in worship. Those who are there are serious in their thoughts. They offer the utmost courtesies to others visiting the garden.

Whether you discover sanctuary in a community garden or in your own plot of land, I know that it takes only the sprinkling of a few extra touches and the right mind-set to capture the serenity that will serve your heart and soul for many days and in many ways.

A stroll through the sanctuary of a garden refuge will let you realize how small you

are compared to the vastness of nature. You will be able to humble yourself while celebrating God's greatness. Say a prayer of thankfulness and take the time to experience the security and gifts of true sanctuary.

A Garden Walk Prayer

Lord, as I meet with You today, may this be a time of encouragement to my soul. I feel so dry inside. My surroundings have been hectic; life isn't working out as I planned; friends have deceived me; and my personal relationships have been thinning. Give me this time to carefully think through all of my tensions. I'm looking for Your peace and tranquility. I praise Your name. Amen.

HE WHO SOWS SPARINGLY WILL ALSO REAP
SPARINGLY; AND HE WHO SOWS BOUNTIFULLY
WILL ALSO REAP BOUNTIFULLY.
—THE BOOK OF 2 CORINTHIANS

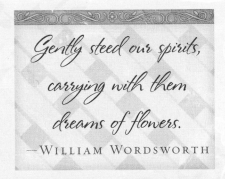

Gently steed our spirits,
carrying with them
dreams of flowers.
—WILLIAM WORDSWORTH

Remember the Birds of the Garden

Make fall a time of plenty for your winged friends who visit the garden in search of food and sanctuary. Birds add beauty and song to your landscape. Here's a fun way for you and the children to keep your feathered friends comfortable and happy all winter long.

1. Use a sharp knife to cut a round squash in half.
2. Scoop out the pulpy insides.
3. Drill 4 small holes around the perimeter and slide thin wooden dowels through the holes. Use dowels long enough to extend as overlapping ends that serve as perches.
4. Wrap wire around the dowels, leaving enough length to hang the improvised feeder from a tree limb, fence, or deck railing. The closer the feeder is to windows, the better your bird watching.
5. Fill the bowl of the squash with the type of bird food that's best for birds in your area. Don't be surprised if the food and the bowl are all eaten.
6. Wintering birds are creatures of habit, so once you begin to feed them, be sure to continue throughout the cold winter months.

TIPS FOR THE GARDENER

Lined latex gloves work just as well in the garden as they do in the kitchen. You don't have any messy fabric gloves to clean—the dirt washes right off rubber gloves. If you put on a little hand lotion before using them, your hands will get a moisturizing treatment while they're pulling weeds and digging in the soil.

GARDEN OF
Nourishment

We also glory in tribulations, knowing that tribulation
produces perseverance; and perseverance, character,
and character, hope. Now hope does not disappoint,
because the love of God has been poured out in our hearts.

—THE BOOK OF ROMANS

There are few joys as great as harvesting your own food. Even if you just have a patio or windowsill, there are myriad fruits and vegetables you can plant in containers. Not only will your body be nourished from the fruits but so will your soul.

I can remember my first garden as a little girl—it was a sweet potato in a mason jar on our kitchen windowsill. That little beginning in our modest home was what motivated me as an adult to plant edible vegetables in our gardens.

What a miracle of God when He takes a little seed, some timely watering, and a little fertilizer, and more vegetables come out of the ground than your family can eat in a season. You don't need a large plot of ground to have a garden of nourishment. In many suburbs, there are community gardens. But if you have a small yard or even a small condo patio or a windowsill, you can still enjoy the harvest.

I challenge you to come away from your rat race, your conveyor belt, your merry-go-round, your traffic jam to be renewed and refreshed in the company of growing things. It won't take long to make the transition, but it will feel like a day in the country. Remember, you're on garden time now. It's time the way God created it: as a servant and not a master.

We "nourishing gardeners" are always in the process of picturing the next phase of our vegetable plots. We are continually assessing what has gone right and what has gone wrong and what might work better next year. Lessons discovered in the fulfillment of our garden dreams are ever-renewing, a source of ongoing energy and passion.

Drying Fresh Herbs

By drying fresh herbs you can preserve their richness for cooking or to enjoy for their scents alone. For large-leafed herbs such as basil, rosemary, and sage, snip off the leafy stems, tie the cut ends together with twine, and hang the bundle upside down in a warm, dry place away from the direct sun and with good circulation. The herbs should be dry and crisp in about two weeks. Strip leaves off of stems and store in an airtight container.

For fine-leafed herbs such as oregano and thyme, remove leaves from stems and spread the leaves on a clean window screen set in a warm, dry, airy place away from the sun. Stir them every few days. Once they feel crisp, store in an airtight container.

Cooking with Herbs

Enjoy the flavor of herbs all year long with these basic recipes.

Bouquet Garni

This little bundle of herbs is a classic ingredient in French cooking. Use to flavor soups and stews. Use fresh herbs whenever possible, tying the stems of the herbs together with a string. But if fresh herbs are not available, you can also use chopped, dried herbs tied in little squares of cheesecloth. Store in tightly covered container:

- 4 sprigs parsley
- 2 sprigs thyme
- 1 bay leaf
- 1 sprig chervil
- 1 sprig marjoram

Use one bundle or packet for every two quarts of soup, and add the herbs about 20 minutes before the soup is done. Before serving, pull out bouquet garni and discard.

Seasoning Herb Mix

This blend of herbs adds delightful flavor to cheese and egg dishes. Again, fresh is best, but you can use dried herbs tied in a cheesecloth bundle.

- 1 sprig each parsley, tarragon, chervil, and chives

Mince finely and add to dish just before serving.

Herbal Salt Substitute

- 1 tablespoon each ground dried basil, coriander, and thyme
- 2 teaspoons each ground cumin, onion powder, and ground dried parsley
- 1 teaspoon each garlic powder, ground mustard, sweet Hungarian paprika, cayenne, and kelp

Mix ingredients and place on table as a salt replacement. Vary herbs and spices to suit your taste.

Tarragon Vinegar

- ⅔ cup tarragon, lightly packed
- 1 cup vinegar

Pick herbs before they flower, and bruise them with the flat of a knife. Place in clear, sterile quart jars and add vinegar. Cover with nonmetal lids and steep for two weeks in a warm, dark place. Shake occasionally. When herbs have steeped, strain vinegar through cheesecloth and discard herbs. Add sprigs of fresh herbs to sterilized bottles and add vinegar. Cork and store in a cool place.

Try other herbs as well (garlic, chive, dill, marjoram, sage, cilantro) and any kind of vinegar you like (experiment with different flavors). Use in salads and sauces. Use the same basic technique to make herbed olive oil.

Tips for the Gardener

Paint the handles of garden tools a bright color so you can spot them easily among the plants and grass. Also, if friends borrow your tools, they will always know where to return them.

"Just living is not enough," said the butterfly. "One must have sunshine, freedom, and a little flower."

—Hans Christian Andersen

*I wonder what
the wind whispers
to the daisies—
making them
ruffle and
twirl about?
My heart smiles
just thinking
about it!*

—KIMBER ANNIE ENGSTROM

HOW COULD
SUCH SWEET AND
WHOLESOME HOURS
BE RECKON'D BUT
WITH HERBS AND
FLOWERS?

—ANDREW MARVELL

Garden of *Thanksgiving*

A single grateful thought toward heaven is the most complete prayer.

—Gotthold Lessing

*O*ne of the great joys in life is to stop and give thanks to God for all of our abundances. We can do it in prayers, in songs, in graces, and in blessings. We can do it for all occasions—births, dedications, housewarmings, graduations, weddings, anniversaries, and many more highlights in our family's life.

These times of gratitude bring us closer together, keep us in touch with God, and help us remember our fellow men and women.

Hubert Simpson said it very well when he prayed:

We thank Thee for the good things of this life, for food and raiment and shelter; for work to do and zest in the doing of it. We thank Thee for the perpetual touch of the divine in life, for the image of Thyself in the soul of man; for the vigor of youth, the wisdom of age, and for all the lessons of experience; the steps by which we climb to higher things; for the courage to be brave, the indignation of the righteous, the kindness of the thoughtful, and all that makes us men and keeps us godlike.

The things that we are most grateful for are not things at all but people, so why not "plant" a scrapbook garden using rocks a child or grandchild colored with paints in a low bed of ground covering, or a collection of shells and rocks collected at beach outings over the years with family and friends. These will be sweet memories for you and for the family.

Paint a word or verse or phrase of gratitude on a stepping-stone, a garden sign, or an ordinary rock that will provide a good surface. Make several of these and place them throughout your garden as reminders to you and your guests to always be grateful.

Slip into your garden this month and pause to thank God for all you have—either in little or abundance. May you be lifted up as you return thanks to God for all He has provided to you and your family.

Storing Up for Spring

I am so grateful for the circle of life, the cycle of seasons. When winter is approaching, invest yourself in the wonderful promise of a future spring by storing some dahlias. Where winters are cold or wet, it's best to remove dahlia tubers from the ground and store them in a frost-free place until spring planting.

In late fall, when foliage has withered, cut back flower stalks to 4-inch stubs. Dig a 2-foot diameter ring around each plant. Gently lift tubers from the ground, shake or hose off soil, and let them dry in the sun for a few hours. Tag them, or use an indelible pen to write the variety name directly on each tuber.

Fill nursery flats or wooden boxes with dry peat moss, sawdust, or wood shavings. Bury the tubers in a single layer. Store in a cool (40° to 50°), dry place until spring planting.

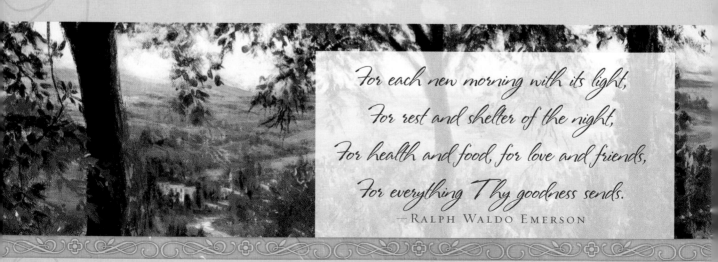

For each new morning with its light,
For rest and shelter of the night,
For health and food, for love and friends,
For everything Thy goodness sends.
—RALPH WALDO EMERSON

Some people always sigh in thanking God.

—Elizabeth B. Browning

Perfect Pumpkin Pie

The coming of winter is an invitation for the garden to settle in and quiet down, but it can be a time of increased warmth and activity in the home as family gatherings fill and brighten our interior spaces. Bring the provision of the garden to those times of celebration with this delicious pumpkin pie. Allow the abundance of creation to bless your times of thanksgiving.

1 ready-made graham pie crust (or you can make your own crust)
1 egg yolk, slightly beaten
1 egg, slightly beaten
1 can (15 ounces) pumpkin mix
1 can (14 ounces) sweetened condensed milk
1 teaspoon cinnamon
½ teaspoon nutmeg
¼ teaspoon salt
¼ teaspoon ginger

Brush bottom and sides of crust with 1 egg yolk. Place on baking sheet. Bake at 350° F for 5 minutes; remove from oven. In large bowl whisk together 1 egg, pumpkin mix, sweetened condensed milk, cinnamon, nutmeg, salt, and ginger until combined. Pour into crust. Bake on baking sheet at 350° F about 50 minutes or until knife inserted in center comes out clean. Cool for 1 hour. Refrigerate at least 2 hours. Garnish with whipped cream. Store in refrigerator.

TIPS FOR THE GARDENER

When planting and planning a garden, seek good advice, even if you don't follow all of it. At first this might seem too costly, but in the long run it will pay big dividends.

- Local nurseries and building supply businesses might provide planning services.
- Talk to experienced gardeners. Check with your local garden, rose, or flower clubs to see if they could be of any help in your renovation. Often this is an excellent resource for the beginner.
- Research, research, research. Not all greenery will grow in all climates. It's best to stick with those plants that have a good track record in your locale.

The Garden of
Celebration

The cheery warmth of the blazing fireplace sets the tone,
and the evergreen smell of the decorated
Christmas tree fills the air along with the music.
We can almost hear the angels singing!

—EMILIE BARNES, *IF TEACUPS COULD TALK*

Whenever it comes to holidays, don't forget your garden when you bring out the decorations. It is as much a part of your home as the indoors. Seasonal lighting, and a planter or planters of colorful flowers help set the mood. Whatever the occasion, use the garden to help you celebrate it.

"The weather outside is frightful, but the fire is so delightful…" The beloved Christmas song "Let It Snow" echoes our sentiments during this snuggle-up time of year. Although it's warm and cozy inside, most of us like to venture out every now and then for wintertime walks and hikes, trips to the mountains, and outdoor fun such as skating and sledding, grateful for the warmth that embraces us when we step back indoors. We all adjust to what we know, and the weather outside gives us yet another hint that Christmas is coming.

If you're an outdoor enthusiast who loves going on nature walks and cross-country ski trips with friends, delighting in the magnificence of the great winter outdoors, then you will enjoy this time of the year. How nice to be able to turn away from the work of your garden and enjoy the gardens that are beyond your fences.

Take this "down time" to enjoy tall trees covered with snow, the abundance of holiday smells, the twinkling of the lights on your home, your Christmas tree, and all the greenery at your local mall. This is a great time to celebrate.

Bundling up and going outdoors puts a touch of pink on your cheeks and a deep appreciation of God's creation in your heart. If you live in a town that regularly gets snow in December, check the phone book for companies that offer sleigh rides. If the ground is dry and the sun is shining, an old-fashioned horse-drawn carriage gives you a similar effect. Long walks through the wintertime woods, an ice-skating party at a nearby pond, or your standard snowman-and-sledding party are all sure to be hits with enthusiastic guests.

Don't wish away the winter days by setting your sights only on a coming season. Find the great pleasure of a slower pace, a calmer spirit, and the holiness of this time.

Grandma Emilie's Strawberry Bread

This is especially good with frozen strawberries from your very own garden. The color, flavor, and scent will remind you of the garden's bounty.

2 cups sugar
3 cups flour
1 teaspoon cinnamon
1 teaspoon baking soda
½ teaspoon salt
2 cups thawed frozen strawberries
1 cup pecans
4 eggs
1¼ cups cooking oil

Mix all ingredients together in a mixing bowl. Grease and flour three 8 x 4 x 2-inch loaf pans. Bake 1 hour at 350°.

Light Up Your Yard with Lanterns

Lanterns should be on everyone's short list of gotta-have decorations. Even though they are a small item, they pack a wallop of a punch to help illuminate your yard at night.

Lanterns are versatile, affordable, and attractive. You can use them in your outdoor decor all year round (yes, even when there is snow all over your yard). You can use them mounted on a wall or as a freestanding accent that gives any display a touch of rustic grandeur.

One reason lanterns are so popular is because they are easy to accessorize. You can display them with a candle or fill them with accents and surround them with florals. No matter what you do, you simply can't go wrong.

Special lighting placed by the front entry is very inviting. Hang or place one lone lantern at the base of your walkway to greet and guide guests to your front door. Another very simple and dramatic way to offer light is to use regular brown lunch sacks as lanterns. Add about 4 inches of sand to the bottom of each bag, place a votive candle on top of the sand and place these bags along your walkway. Before your holiday guests arrive, light the candles. Your guests will be impressed with the illuminated effect.

No matter where you put your lanterns, they will be sure to light up your life.

Winter Special Potpourri

In a large jar, combine 2 cups each of rose petals, rosemary, and mint with ½ cup whole allspice, 4 cinnamon sticks, and 2 garlic cloves. Fill the jar with hot white distilled vinegar to cover. Cover the jar and let it set for one week. The longer the herbs soak, the stronger the scent. Experiment with your favorite fragrant blossoms and herbs such as lavender, lemon verbena, or sage.

Soak cotton balls in the wet potpourri. When dry, they make simple sachets for lingerie or linens. You can also use the liquid mix in an atomizer to spray as a room deodorizer or leave the jar uncapped for an old-fashioned room scent.

> THE BEST OF ALL GIFTS AROUND ANY CHRISTMAS TREE: THE PRESENCE OF A HAPPY FAMILY ALL WRAPPED UP IN EACH OTHER.
>
> —BURTON HILLIS

Tips for the Gardener

If you buy a container-grown conifer, here's how to keep it healthy during its indoor stay, which should be limited to ten days.

- Keep the tree in its plastic nursery can. Place it in a cool spot away from heat sources. Put a saucer underneath to catch any water drips.
- Hide the nursery can and saucer by slipping them into a decorative container or wrapping them with holiday-colored fabric.
- Decorate with small, cool-burning lights. To water, dump two trays of ice cubes on top of the soil daily. As the ice melts, water trickles slowly down through the root zone.

Light gives of itself freely, filling all available space. It does not seek anything in return; it asks not whether you are friend or foe. It gives of itself and is not thereby diminished.

—Michael Strassfeld

CHRISTMAS,
CHILDREN,
IS NOT A DATE.
IT IS A STATE
OF MIND.

—MARY ELLEN CHASE

We must cultivate our garden.
—Voltaire

I WILL BE THE GLADDEST THING UNDER THE SUN!
I WILL TOUCH A HUNDRED FLOWERS
AND NOT PICK ONE.

—Edna St. Vincent Millay